Contents

The Great Fire of London

▼ A very long time ago,
London looked like this.

The old city of London was
burned in a great fire.
This happened almost
350 years ago.

4
.....   ago   old   burned   fire   years

START-UP
HISTORY

◀ • • • • • • • • • • • ▶

The Great Fire of London

Stewart Ross

W

Franklin Watts

Copyright © White-Thomson Publishing 2016

All rights reserved.

ISBN 978 1 4451 3501 4

A CIP catalogue record for this book is
available from the British Library.

Editor: Anna Lee
Consultant: Norah Granger
Designer: Tessa Barwick
Map Illustration: The Map Studio
Packaged by: White-Thomson Publishing www.wtpub.co.uk

This book was first published by Evans Brothers Ltd. It has been revised and fully updated in line with the KS1 History curriculum.

Picture credits
Key: t=top, b=bottom, l=left, r=right

Cover: Wikimedia (all); p1 The Great Fire of London, 1666 (print) (see also 53641), Verschuier, Lieve (1630-86) (after)/Private Collection / Bridgeman Images; p4 l Old London Bridge, detail from 'Vischer's London', 17th century (engraving), Visscher, Nicolaes (Claes) Jansz (1586-1652)/Private Collection / Bridgeman Images; pp4–5 The Great Fire of London, 1666 (print) (see also 53641), Verschuier, Lieve (1630-86) (after)/Private Collection / Bridgeman Images; p5 r View of the Monument, c.1770, James, William (1730-80)/Private Collection/Photo © Gavin Graham Gallery, London, UK/Bridgeman Images; p7 t Wikimedia; p7 b The Great Fire of London in 1666 (oil on panel), Dutch School, (17th century)/© Museum of London, UK/Bridgeman Images; p8 l Wikimedia; p8 r Wikimedia; p9 Wikimedia; p10 Mary Evans Picture Library; p11 Mary Evans Picture Library; p12 Topham Picturepoint; p13 Shutterstock/Ron Ellis; p14 Bridgeman; p15 Topham/PA; pp 16–17 Wikimedia; p18 l Portrait of Sir Christopher Wren (oil on canvas), English School, (18th century)/Private Collection/Bridgeman Images; pp18–19 St. Paul's Cathedral before it was destroyed by the Fire of London from 'A Book of the Prospects of the Remarkable Places in and about the City of London', c.1700 (engraving), Morden, Robert (fl.1682-1703)/O'Shea Gallery, London, UK/Bridgeman Images; p19 r North East view of St. Paul's Cathedral, c.1850 (litho), English School, (19th century)/London Metropolitan Archives, City of London/Bridgeman Images; p20 l Wikimedia; p20 r North East view of St. Paul's Cathedral, c.1850 (litho), English School, (19th century)/London Metropolitan Archives, City of London/Bridgeman Images; p21 l Wikimedia; p21 tr Mary Evans Picture Library; p21 br The Great Fire of London, 1666 (print) (see also 53641), Verschuier, Lieve (1630-86) (after)/Private Collection / Bridgeman Images.

Printed in China

Franklin Watts
An imprint of
Hachette Children's Group
Part of The Watts Publishing Group
Carmelite House
50 Victoria Embankment
London EC4Y 0DZ

An Hachette UK Company
www.hachette.co.uk

www.franklinwatts.co.uk

Every effort has been made by the Publishers to ensure that the websites in this book are suitable for children, and that they contain no inappropriate or offensive material. However, because of the nature of the Internet, it is impossible to guarantee that the contents of these sites will not be altered. We strongly advise that Internet access is supervised by a responsible adult.

▼ These people watched the flames from boats on the River Thames.

After the fire, the city was rebuilt.

▲ This Monument was built so that people remember the Great Fire. It is still standing today.

flames   river   rebuilt   today

When was the Great Fire of London?

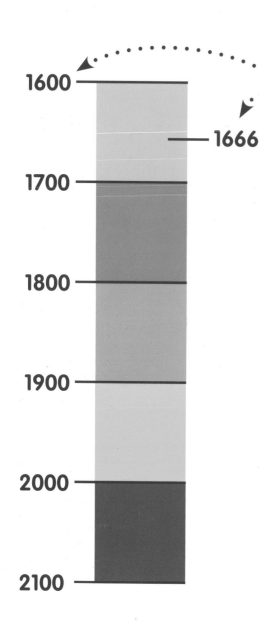

1600

1666

1700

1800

1900

2000

2100

These numbers are years.
We also call them dates.
What is the date today?

100 years is called a century.
In the timeline each century
is a different colour.

The Great Fire of London
was in the year 1666.

dates   century

◄ This is King Charles II.
He was the King
of England in 1666.

▼ Here is a painting of the fire.
Is it night-time or daytime?
Paintings like this tell us
about the fire.

timeline   painting

How do we know about the Great Fire?

▶ **This is Samuel Pepys. He lived in London at the time of the Great Fire. He wrote about the fire in his diary.**

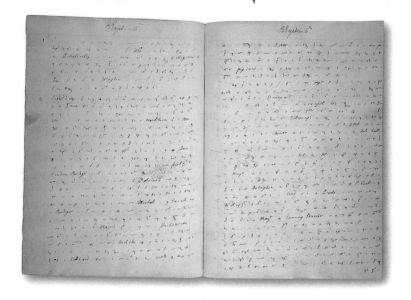

"It made me weep to see it. The churches, houses, and all on fire and flaming at once, and a horrid noise the flames made."

diary   churches

◀ **This is John Evelyn. He also wrote about the fire in his diary.**

"By night it was light as day for ten miles round about."

People who watch an event are called 'eyewitnesses'. Samuel Pepys and John Evelyn were eyewitnesses to the Great Fire.

houses   miles   eyewitnesses

How did the Great Fire start?

The Great Fire **began** with a little fire in a **bakery**.

The bakery was in a street called Pudding Lane.

In this picture of a bakery from the **past**, the fire is inside the **oven**.

began   bakery   past

The houses of old London
were very close to each other.
How did the fire spread from
the bakery to other houses?

oven   spread   11
· · · ·

Why did a little fire become the Great Fire?

These houses are from the time of the Great Fire.

They are built with wood frames.
We call them timber-framed.

This type of house burns easily.

wood   timber-framed

These **Victorian** houses are made of **bricks** and **plaster**.
This type of house does not burn easily.

During the Great Fire the **wind** sent the flames from
one house to another.
Pepys thought the fire would reach his house,
so he moved out.

Victorian   bricks   plaster   wind   **13**

Trying to put out the fire

There was no fire brigade at the time of the Great Fire.

People had to carry water from the River Thames in buckets. It took a long time.

They could not put out the big fire.

fire brigade   buckets

◄ Firefighters today have fire engines to carry their hoses and ladders. They can stop a fire spreading to other houses.

After the Great Fire

The Great Fire of London **lasted** for five days.
It burned 13,200 houses.

Cathedral of S. Paul

THE RIVER

The top picture shows what London looked like
before the fire.

16

lasted **before**

The bottom picture shows what it looked like afterwards.

Many people had no homes.
Pepys' house was not burned down.

You can see that many churches were still standing.
Why were they not destroyed?

afterwards   homes   destroyed   **17**

Building a new city

▼ This is Christopher Wren. He planned a pleasant new London with wide streets and houses made of stone and brick.

The old London was crowded and dirty. The new city was cleaner and healthier.

18

planned   streets   stone   crowded

▼ Before the fire, St Paul's Cathedral was the most famous building in London. After the fire, it was a ruin.

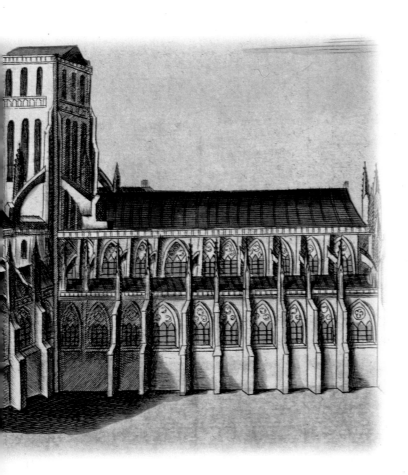

▲ Christopher Wren built the new St Paul's Cathedral. How is it different from the old one? It is still standing today, but parts of it have changed.

dirty   cleaner   healthier   ruin

Here is a map of London in 1666. The yellow, orange and red areas burned down.

Use these pictures to tell the story of the Great Fire.

KEY

	London
	Area burned on Sunday, 2nd September, 1666
	Area burned on Monday, 3rd September, 1666
	Area burned on Tuesday/Wednesday, 4/5th September, 1666
	London Wall, which was built long ago and surrounded the city of London.

ALDERSGATE STREET

HOLBORN

FETTER LANE

LUDGATE HILL

St Paul's Cathedral

RIVER

the Great Fire

N
W   E
S

0   250   500
metres

BISHOPSGATE STREET

WHITECHAPEL

CHEAPSIDE

CORNHILL

LOMBARD STREET

SEETHING LANE
(Pepys' street)

TOWER STREET

THAMES STREET

The Tower
of
London

LONDON BRIDGE

PUDDING LANE

THAMES

New history words and words about the Fire of London listed in the text:

ago	cleaner	firefighters	oven	streets
afterwards	crowded	flames	painting	timber-framed
bakery	dates	healthier	past	timeline
before	destroyed	homes	planned	today
began	diary	hoses	plaster	Victorian
bricks	dirty	houses	rebuilt	wind
buckets	engines	ladders	river	wood
burned	eyewitnesses	lasted	ruin	years
century	fire	miles	spread	
churches	fire brigade	old	stone	

Background Information

THE GREAT FIRE

The fire raged from 2 to 6 September 1666, early in the reign of Charles II. It was blamed (falsely) on foreigners, especially the Dutch (with whom the country was at war) and the Catholic French. The blaze destroyed 89 churches as well as St Paul's. The fire began at a baker's in Pudding Lane and the Monument was erected near there. Plans for a wholly new city were rejected, but parliament did regulate to make further fires less likely (stipulating building materials, etc.). Significantly, the city was never again smitten with an outbreak of plague as virulent as that of 1665.

CHARLES II

The fire took place during the reign of Charles II (1660-1685), son of the executed Charles I. The king was at Westminster when the fire broke out. He showed some alacrity in ordering houses in the path of the flames to be pulled down or blown up. Memory of the disastrous fire, widely blamed on Catholics, fuelled the Exclusion Crisis of 1679-81, when parliament attempted to bar the king's brother, the Roman Catholic James Duke of York, from the succession.

CHRISTOPHER WREN

Sir Christopher Wren (1632-1723) became surveyor-general of the king's works in 1669. He developed a passionate interest in architecture and was the principal architect for the rebuilding of London after the fire.

SAMUEL PEPYS

A sharp-witted civil servant, Samuel Pepys (1633-1703) served as Secretary to the Admiralty from 1672-9 and 1684-88. Pepys' candid record of his life between 1660 and 1669 was written in a form of shorthand that was not deciphered until 1825. Often published, (sometimes bowdlerised), it has established itself as a popular literary classic and an invaluable and accessible source of information on Restoration England.

Parents and Teachers

JOHN EVELYN

After fighting for the king during the Civil War (1642-48), Evelyn (1620-1706) travelled abroad. He returned with Charles II and became a familiar figure at court and a founder member of the Royal Society. A collector and patron of the arts, he wrote a number of works besides his famous diary.

ST PAUL'S CATHEDRAL

The 'Old St Paul's', left in ruins by the Great Fire, was begun in Norman times and completed in the fourteenth century. It was the longest building in Britain and the third longest cathedral in Europe. After the fire, the cathedral was patched up for services. However, subsequent structural collapses persuaded the authorities to start again. Work on the new building, designed by Christopher Wren, began in 1675 and was completed in 1708, 42 years after the Great Fire.

Possible Activities:

Read selected and edited passages from Pepys diary.
Discuss the role of eyewitnesses in historical events.
Write diaries.
Draw pictures of the fire.
Make a class frieze timeline.
Compare the map on pages 20-21 with a map of London today.

Some Topics for Discussion:

Which tells us more about the fire, Pepys or a painting?
Why did the fire start /stop?
The role of the River Thames (escape route / barrier, etc.).
How did London benefit from the Great Fire?

Further Information

BOOKS

FOR CHILDREN

The Danger Zone: Avoid Being in the Great Fire of London by Jim Pipe (Book House, 2010)
The Great Fire of London Unclassified: Secrets Revealed by Nick Hunter (National Archives, 2013)
Popcorn History Corner: The Great Fire of London by Jenny Powell (Wayland, 2011)
Ways into History: The Great Fire of London by Sally Hewitt (Watts, 2012)

FOR ADULTS

The Great Fire of London by Stephen Porter (The History Press, 2009)
London - the Biography by Peter Ackroyd (Vintage, 2001)
Samuel Pepys: the Unequalled Self by Claire Tomalin (Penguin, 2003)

WEBSITES

http://www.everyschool.co.uk/history-key-stage-1-fire-of-london.html
http://www.theschoolrun.com/homework-help/great-fire-london
http://www.fireoflondon.org.uk
http://www.bbc.co.uk/history/british/civil_war_revolution/great_fire_01.shtml
http://www.pepys.info/fire.html

PLACES TO VISIT

The Museum of London
The Monument, London
St Paul's Cathedral

Index